W9-BZU-404

Scrapbooking

Keep Your Special Memories

by Deborah Hufford

Capstone press

Mankato, Minnesota

Snap Books are published by Capstone Press,
151 Good Counsel Drive, P.O. Box 669, Mankato, Minnesota 56002
www.capstonepress.com

Library of Congress Cataloging-in-Publication Data
Hufford, Deborah.
Scrapbooking: keep your special memories / by Deborah Hufford.
p. cm. -- (Snap books crafts)
Includes bibliographical references and index.
ISBN 0-7368-4387-6 (hardcover: alk. paper)
1. Photographs--Conservation and restoration--Juvenile literature.
2. Photograph albums--Juvenile literature. 3. Scrapbooks--Juvenile literature.
4. Children--Collectibles--Juvenile literature. 5. Teenagers--Collectibles--Juvenile literature.
I. Title. II. Series.
TR465.H84 2006
745.593--dc22   2005006901

Summary: A do-it-yourself crafts book for children and pre-teens on scrapbooking.

Editors: Thea Feldman; Deb Berry/Bill SMITH STUDIO
Illustrators: Lisa Parett; Roxanne Daner, Marina Terletsky and Brock Waldron/Bill SMITH STUDIO
Designers: Roxanne Daner, Marina Terletsky, and Brock Waldron/Bill SMITH STUDIO
Photo Researcher: Iris Wong/Bill SMITH STUDIO

Photo Credits: Cover: (girl) Getty Images & Richard Hutchings Photography; 4 (t) Eyewire Images, (frame) Ingram Publishing, (b) Bill Smith; 5 (frame) PhotoDisc, (tl) Bill Smith, (tr) PhotoDisc, (b) PhotoDisc; 6 (all) PhotoDisc; 7 (tl) Ingram Publishing, (bl & br) Richard Hutchings Photography; 8-9 PhotoDisc; 10-11 Corel; 11 (r) Photographer's Choice/Getty Images, (frame) Eyewire; 12-13 Richard Hutchings; 14 PhotoDisc; 15 (bc) Richard Hutchings Photography; 17 PhotoDisc; 18 (inset) PhotoDisc, (bg) Richard Hutchings Photography; 19 Richard Hutchings Photography; 20 Bill Smith; 21 (tc, l, r) Bill Smith (tr) Ingram Publishing; 22 (tr) PhotoDisc, (bc) Richard Hutchings Photography; 23 (inset) Bill Smith, (bg) Richard Hutchings Photography; 24-25 (fg) DigitalVision; 25 (tl) Corel, (c) PhotoDisc, (r) Eyewire; 26 (bl) PhotoDisc; 27 (c) Eyewire, (cl) DigitalVision, (tl, bl) PhotoDisc, (cr) Bill Smith STUDIO, (bg) Richard Hutchings Photography; 28-29 PhotoDisc; 32(tr) Courtesy Deborah Hufford.

1 2 3 4 5 6 10 09 08 07 06 05

Table of Contents

CHAPTER 1 History in the Making 4

CHAPTER 2 A Work of Art 6

CHAPTER 3 Turning Memories into Magic 8

CHAPTER 4 Friendly Reminder 10

CHAPTER 5 Creature Comforts 14

CHAPTER 6 Weave a Childhood Tale 16

CHAPTER 7 Past Perfect 20

CHAPTER 8 Rock, Paper, Scissors 24

Fast Facts 28

Glossary 30

Read More 31

Internet Sites 31

About the Author 32

Index 32

Go Metric!

It's easy to change measurements to metric! Just use this chart.

To change	into	multiply by
inches	centimeters	2.54
inches	millimeters	25.4
feet	meters	.305
yards	meters	.914
ounces (liquid)	milliliters	29.57
ounces (liquid)	liters	.029
cups (liquid)	liters	.237
pints	liters	.473
quarts	liters	.946
gallons	liters	3.78
ounces (dry)	grams	28.35
pounds	grams	453.59

CHAPTER 1

History in the Making

Keep a scrapbook of your own "story."

You may think you lead a pretty normal life with school, family, and friends. But did you ever think of yourself as making history? Well, you are! The history of your very own life. Now you can save the memories of the most important moments in your life with a scrapbook.

This book will teach you how to showcase the people, places, and events that matter most to you in a decorative scrapbook that is fun and easy to create.

So Many Scrapbooks!

You can get all kinds of scrapbooks for everything from school to sports, hobbies to holidays, pets to parties. Some even have fancy covers and lockets. You can also design your own cover.

Scrapbook

CHAPTER 2

A Work of Art

Turn your piles of photos into works of art.

Do you have stacks of photographs, school papers, and precious little things stuffed in drawers and boxes? Well, now you can turn those messy piles into scrapbook art.

The first step is to get everything into neat piles so you know what you have. Here are some tips.

1 Divide your favorite **photographs** by year or grade and label the backs with a soft-tip **photo-safe marker**.

2 Store photos in envelopes or shoeboxes, using **acid-free paper** as backing. This will keep the color from fading and the paper from getting ruined.

Once you've got everything in order, all that's left to do is to start scrapbooking.

Be a Copycat

Preserve your valuable photographs by taking them to a copy shop to have color copies made. You can also size them to fit your scrapbook pages.

Marvelous Mattes

Scrapbookers often use mattes to decorate photographs. You can find mattes at craft stores or make your own using decorative paper, ribbon, lace, or beading.

CHAPTER 3

Turning Memories into Magic

Get the tools you need, and get going.

All the designs in this book work best in a scrapbook at least 11 inches by 11 inches. You'll also need scissors, a ruler, a photo-safe marker, a glue stick, and colored markers.

Safety First

Look for this box for safety tips for each project. Remember, safety first and fun will follow.

Pick a Pack of Paper

Decorative papers come in lots of wonderful patterns and colors. Here are some tips on picking the right ones.

- If the photo is too "busy," use a solid colored paper.

- If the photo is too plain, use a paper with a pattern. Got a picture of yourself in a plain white dress? Try paper with pink polka dots to liven it up.

- If the photo was taken on a holiday, use paper that fits the holiday. For example, you can use red, white, and blue paper for the Fourth of July, or red and pink for Valentine's Day.

CHAPTER 4

Friendly Reminder

Make a special page for your best friends.

Decorate favorite photos of friends and arrange them on a scrapbook page. You'll smile every time you open your scrapbook and see their faces. And your friends will be thrilled that you've included them in your beautiful scrapbook!

Here's what you need

* scrapbook page
* glue stick
* 11-inch by 11-inch decorative paper
* 2 yards, ½-inch-wide satin ribbon
* scissors
* ruler
* pencil
* 5½-inch by 7½-inch white **cardstock**
* 6-inch by 8-inch black cardstock
* 5-inch by 7-inch photograph
* black fine-tip marker
* two 1-inch by 3-inch tags
* one 2-inch by 6-inch tag
* six **brads**

Here's what you do

1 Glue decorative paper to scrapbook page to create background.

2 Glue ribbon around edges of paper.

3 Mark middle of paper's top edge with a pencil dot, and repeat on each side.

4 Glue ribbon from one dot to another to create a crisscross pattern, then trim.

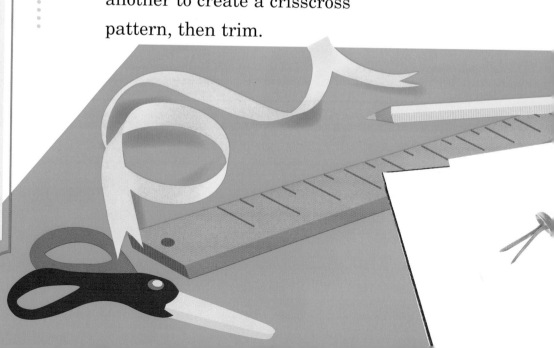

5 Center white cardstock on black cardstock and glue.

6 Center photograph on white cardstock and glue.

7 Center matted photograph on scrapbook page, and glue so tips of corners are tucked underneath ribbons.

8 Hand letter tags and glue on background.

9 Glue brads on tags.

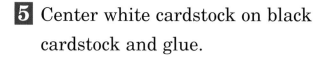

Crisscrossing Paths

Have you ever gone into a photo booth with a friend and made goofy faces for the camera? You can matte these little photos and place them inside the smaller crisscrossed ribbons.

JEN 2006

EMMA 2006

CHAPTER 5

Creature Comforts

Make scrapbooking a "pet" project.

Designing a pet page is especially fun. There are so many fun animal decorations for scrapbooking. This project uses special paper with cat or dog designs, pet tags, and charms. Even if you don't have a pet, you can still design a page or two of your favorite animal.

Here's what you need

* scrapbook page
* 11-inch by 11-inch decorative animal paper
* glue stick
* 3½-inch by 5-inch pet or animal photo
* 4-inch by 5½-inch card stock
* black fine-tip marker
* scissors
* small pet collar (or 5-inch strip of leather and a buckle)
* 1-inch by 3-inch tag
* three metal pet tags or animal charms

Here's what you do

1. Glue decorative paper to scrapbook page to create background.

2. Glue cardstock in middle of paper.

3. Center photograph on cardstock and glue.

4. Glue collar or leather strip with buckle across top of photo.

5. Write pet's or animal's name on tag and glue above collar.

6. Glue metal tags or charms at bottom edge of photograph.

REMEMBER!

Safety First

Keep small scrapbooking items such as charms and pet tags away from young children and pets to prevent accidents.

Stamp of Approval

Custom-make your own patterned paper by stamping. For a pet layout, stamp paw prints using different colors of inks.

CHAPTER 6

Weave a Childhood Tale

Sometimes it's good to baby yourself.

Weave your favorite baby picture into a scrapbook page. This decorative treatment looks fancy but is quick, easy, and fun.

ABCs of Scrapbooking

Scrapbookers often use decorative tags for important titles or notes. Buy tags or make them by drawing borders on white paper.

A Note About Picking Papers

For a more exciting scrapbook page, choose one solid-colored paper, and another with a pattern, like stripes, flowers, or checkerboard.

Here's what you need

* 12-inch by 12-inch scrapbook page
* 11-inch by 11-inch white paper
* four sheets of 8- to 12-inch by 11-inch decorative papers in two colors or patterns
* spray **adhesive**
* ruler
* scissors
* glue stick
* baby photograph
* oval or round matte frame
* 12 inches of ½-inch-wide satin ribbon
* black fine-tip marker
* two 2-inch by 3½-inch tags

Here's what you do

1 Glue white paper to scrapbook page.

2 Spray adhesive on white paper.

3 Cut the decorative papers into 1-inch by 11-inch strips.

4 Starting at the top of the scrapbook page, glue alternating strips of paper going all the way down the page.

5 Beginning at left edge of paper, "weave" alternating strips of paper through the strips from Step 4. This will create a criss-cross pattern.

6 Trim photograph to fit in matte frame.

7 Glue frame and photograph in center of page.

8 Cut four 1½-inch-long ribbon pieces.

9 Wrap each ribbon piece around corner of woven background and glue on back.

10 Tie bow with 6 inches of ribbon, and glue above photograph.

11 Hand letter tags, putting your full name on one and your date, time, and place of birth on the other.

12 Center tags on page and glue.

REMEMBER!

SPRAY

! Safety First
When using spray adhesive, always follow directions. Use in an open area and spray away from face. Be careful to keep spray away from your eyes and nose.

CHAPTER 7

Past Perfect

Black-and-white photographs capture a "colorful" past.

This project shows you how to decorate old photographs with beautiful paper patterns and metal charms.

You'll make the past come back to life in a blaze of color!

Here's what you need

* 12-inch by 12-inch scrapbook page
* 8½-inch by 11-inch cardstock, any color
* ruler
* pencil
* three 8½-inch by 11-inch contrasting decorative cloths or papers, one the same color as ribbons
* 4½-inch by 6½-inch decorative paper
* scissors
* glue stick
* 4-inch by 6-inch black-and-white photo
* two pieces of 4-inch-long decorative ribbon
* two metal charms, different sizes

Here's what you do

1 Glue cardstock onto scrapbook page.

2 Cut one decorative sheet to 8½ inches by 4 inches, and glue across top of cardstock.

3 Cut second decorative sheet to 8½ inches by 7 inches and glue across bottom of cardstock.

4 Cut decorative sheet that matches ribbon to 4½ inches by 6½ inches.

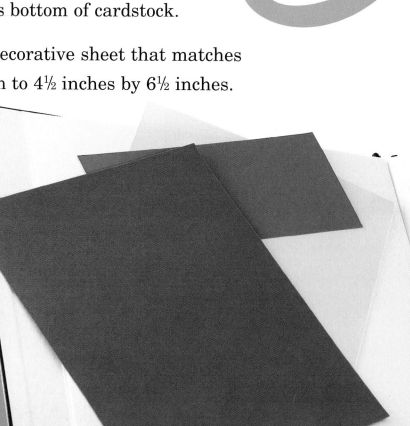

5. Center and glue photograph onto decorative paper from Step 4.

6. Glue photo and paper onto center of scrapbook page.

7. Glue ribbon on each side of photograph, covering line where contrasting patterns meet.

8. Glue ribbon ends to back of scrapbook page.

9. Glue larger charm above photograph, smaller one below.

Age Your Photos in a Flash

Turn color photographs into black-and-whites or sepia-tones by adjusting the color balance on a color copier. Ask an attendant at a photocopy center for help. Color copies usually cost $1 to $3 per page.

CHAPTER 8

Rock, Paper, Scissors

Some memories seem written in stone. Capture them on paper, too.

Looking at vacation pictures is like taking the trip all over again without leaving home.

This project features a vacation to Mount Rushmore. But you can use these tips for any vacation, even if it's just tenting in your own backyard.

U.S. MAIL

Here's what you need

* scrapbook page
* 11-inch by 11-inch decorative paper
* three to five vacation photographs
* two to five vacation souvenirs (such as postcards, dried flowers, tickets, maps, or coins)
* one or two, 2-inch by 3½-inch tags
* glue stick
* scissors
* black fine-tip marker
* bits of cloth
* buttons

Here's what you do

1 Glue decorative paper to scrapbook page to create background. Hand letter a tag with title.

2 Arrange title tag and several photographs as desired on page, then arrange souvenirs, cloth, and buttons around them.

3 Glue all pieces in place.

Pocketful of Posies

Scrapbook pockets are cute and fill a useful purpose. They hold loose items you don't have room for on the page. Cut a back pocket from old blue jeans, glue onto the paper, and tuck some dried flowers into the pocket.

MY VACATION

MOUNT RUSHMORE NATIONAL MEMORIAL

Fast Facts

The Birth of Scrapbooking

Ever since the invention of photography in the 1830s, people have been collecting family photos. When they started keeping them in books along with letters, notes, and other souvenirs, scrapbooking was born.

Mark Twain's Favorite Hobby

Mark Twain is most famous for writing *The Adventures of Tom Sawyer* and *The Adventures of Huckleberry Finn*. But his best-selling book while he was alive was his *Mark Twain's Patent Scrapbook*, which he invented in 1872. It was very popular with scrapbookers because it had a built-in adhesive on the pages. It sold over 25,000 copies!

Memories Are Golden

Some people think of old family scrapbooks as valuable pieces of history. They study them to understand what people's everyday lives were like.

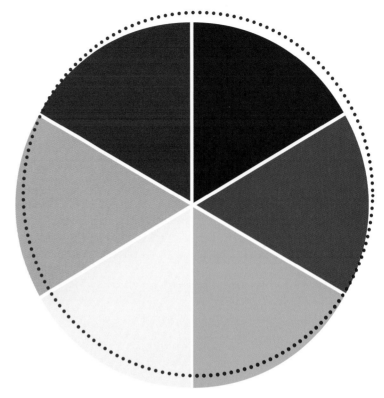

Color Wheel

When creating scrapbooks, color is key. This wheel shows how colors work with each other. The colors next to each other work together in harmony. Colors opposite each other have a stronger effect when used together because they have more contrast.

Glossary

acid-free paper (ASS-id-FREE PAY-pur) paper that does not contain acid that ruins the color of the photos and even the photo paper itself

adhesive (ad-HEE-siv) a liquid, gel, or paste that holds things together, such as glue

brad (BRAD) decorative metal piece that looks a bit like a nailhead

cardstock (KARD-stok) paper about the weight of postcard paper

decorative (DEK-ur-uh-tiv) a word to describe anything that makes something look prettier or more exciting

matte (MAT) a decorative border around a picture

photographs (FOH-tuh-grafs) pictures that are taken with a camera (called "photos" for short)

photo-safe marker (FOH-toh SAYF MARK-uhr) acid-free, felt-tip marker used for labeling backs of photographs

sepia-tone (SEE-pee-uh TOHN) a brownish tint that is added to black-and-white photographs

Read More

American Girl. *My Life!: Scrapbook Kit.* Middleton, Wisconsin: American Girl, 2001.

Haglund, Jill and Kerry Arquette. *Scrapbooking for Kids, Ages 1 to 100.* Sarasota, Florida: Tweety Jill Publications, Inc., 1999.

Larsen, Nikki. *Scribbles, Stickers & Glue: A Kids' Guide to Scrapbooking.* New York: Sterling/Chapelle, 2004.

Scholastic Books. *My School Memories: A Scrapbooking Kit.* New York: Scholastic, 1999.

Schuh, Debby and Julie Stephani. *Kids' Scrapbooking: Easy As 1-2-3.* Iola, Wisconsin: Krause Publications, 2002.

Internet Sites

FactHound offers a safe, fun way to find Internet sites related to this book. All of the sites on FactHound have been researched by our staff.

Here's how

1. Visit *www.facthound.com*

2. Type in this special code **0736843876** for age-appropriate sites. Or enter a search word related to this book for a more general search.

3. Click on the **Fetch It** button. FactHound will fetch the best sites for you!

About the Author

Deborah Hufford was a staff writer for *Country Home* and the former editor of *Country Handcrafts* magazine, which included a regular craft column called "Kids' Korner." She was also the crafts editor for *McMagazine,* a magazine created for McDonald's Corporation. Most recently she served as the associate publisher for two of the country's leading craft magazines, *Bead & Button* and *Dollhouse Miniatures*, as well as a book division of crafts titles.

Index

acid-free paper, 7

baby photo, 18
beading, 7
blue jeans, 27
brads, 12, 13
buckle, 15
buttons, 26

cardstock, 12-15, 22
charms, 14, 15, 20, 22, 23

decorative papers, 9, 15, 22, 26

frame, 18, 19

glue stick, 8, 12, 14, 18, 22, 26

lace, 7
leather strips, 14, 15

markers, 8, 14, 15, 18, 26
mattes, 7

paper, 7, 9, 14, 15, 17, 18, 23
patterns, 9, 12, 15, 17, 20
paw print stamp, 15
pencil, 22
pet collar, 14, 15
pet photo, 14, 15
photos, 6, 7, 9, 10, 13, 18-20, 23, 26
photo-safe marker, 7, 8

ribbon, 7, 12, 13, 18, 19, 22, 23
ruler, 8, 12, 18, 22

safety, 9, 15, 19
scissors, 8, 12, 14, 18, 22, 26
spray adhesive, 18

tags, 17-19, 26

vacation souvenirs, 26